First published in 1995 by Virgin Books
an imprint of Virgin Publishing Limited
332 Ladbroke Grove
London W10 5AH

Designed and produced for Virgin Publishing
by Cooling Brown, Hampton, Middlesex, England
Edited, written and designed by
Tony Horkins, Vici McCarthy and Arthur Brown

Cover photography by Philip Ollerenshaw
All photography by Philip Ollerenshaw except
pp2, 3, 4(middle), 16, 17, 18, 19, 20(except middle left), 21, 24,
27(bottom right), 35 by Tom Howard, p20(middle left), p33(middle) by Moy Williams,
pp44, 45(top) by Robert Walker.

ISBN: 185227 558 8
Printed and bound by The Bath Press, Great Britain

ntents

tour photographer tom howard spills the beans on Take That

a sneaky peek at rehearsals for the european tour

the fuss and furore over howard's cheeky costume

including hairstyles. at the salon with mark and co

who knows all about the latest album sleeve? **nobody else**
but designer morgan penn

Take That pick up an award... or ten

how well do you **really** *know the That?*

*they've got the whole world in their hands... and we prise
open their fingers*

the princes of pop meet the Prince and Princess of Wales

a spooky, astrological rummage into Take That's future

on his new health plan: "I've made a conscious effort to lose weight. I was spurred into action after seeing my *Spitting Image* puppet, which was completely unflattering. Jason is a complete health freak and he's been supervising my diet."

on being happy: "Someone told me that if you add together the sales of every single from number two to number 18 at the moment and then double that it won't come anywhere near to the sales for *Back For Good* – and you can't say you're not happy with that!"

on his self-image: "Being constantly surrounded by four muscly good-looking blokes makes me paranoid."

on a possible solo career: "That's rubbish. I'm not leaving."

on being a rock'n'roll demon: "After a gig I get to the hotel all psyched-up from being on stage and get stuck into *Homes and Interiors* magazine!"

on his home life: "I have a German Shepherd dog. Her name's Jess and she's a year old. The apartment we live in is quite small but it's big enough for me and Jess!"

on penny watching: "I want to be remembered as a good pop star who later retired to good living."

on fan loyalty: "Our fan base is so brilliant in the UK that if we put out a record with burping on it it would probably be a hit, but we're not just in it for the hits. We want to make something of quality."

on recording *Nobody Else* in his own studio: "I know I have a reputation for being a tightwad but it was done for practical reasons. It just goes to show that you don't need to spend a fortune. It's quality that sells the music, nothing less.

on having lottery tickets bought for him by a fan!: "I'll see how faithful she is if they come up!"

on ghosts!: "I have seen a ghost. I was 15 and playing at a Manchester theatre when me and my mate saw a woman in the corridor hovering above the ground. She went straight through my mate and disappeared."

on writing *Nobody Else* for his parents: "I was home at Christmas and my mum and dad were in the loft looking through old photos of themselves. I began to think about the hopes they must have had when they were young and how their lives turned out to be pretty good. They've got two sons doing well for themselves and they're still in love and still happy."

"I want to be remembered as a good pop star who later retired to a good living."

on Christmas: "I cooked Christmas dinner for my mate and his girlfriend and I was on the phone to my mother every half an hour to find out what to do next. I had me turkey in the oven and I kept phoning her to find out how to make the gravy, 'cause it was the hardest thing to do. I'd done the whole meal and eaten it when I realised that I'd forgotten to put the gravy on. It was on the side in this little pot. I was gutted."

on his socks: "I always smell 'em first and if they don't smell too much then I'll wear em."

on dislocating his finger (the buffoon): "I've never known pain like it!"

on his social life: "On average I go to a club about once a month when I'm at home, but I go out much more when I'm abroad or away with the band. I prefer just to go out with really good mates. We usually go club-crawling — going to a few until we find one we like that's playing the right music."

on wishes: "I'd love to see my grandfather again. He died two years ago. Because Take That were becoming successful I had a really busy time and didn't manage to see him as much as I'd have liked to in his last year. I'd have a lot to talk to him about if I saw him now."

on ambitions: "I want to get more knowledge of my studio — I've just got a new studio and I intend to spend more time there."

on piercing: "I really wanted to get my nipple pierced but that's it. I'm stopping now!"

on home life: "I still live with my parents but I'm not in any hurry to move. I love my room. I've got everything in there. I've got me sink! I've got a kettle up there for whenever I want to make a brew! My keyboards are up there. The colour scheme is very beige with a bit of deep green, and I've got a single bed 'cause I can't sleep in a double bed... unless it's got a girl in it!"

on the future of Take That: "I hope we'll still be together in five years."

on the release of Back For Good: "I think it was quite scary when Back For Good came out because there had been such a big gap between us releasing singles. We weren't sure how people would take it."

on his bare bum!: "I think the papers in Europe aren't so bothered about it like the papers in Britain. I couldn't believe it when it actually made the front cover of newspapers. In Europe they see more naked flesh in magazines, it's more natural."

"I've never known pain like it…"

on his diet: "I eat chicken, turkey and fish, so maybe I'm not that strict. But I don't eat red meat – I cut it from my diet purely for health reasons. I eat well, though – I try to eat as many raw vegetables as I can. Oh... and I make a mean curry!"

on home life: "I will live wherever I feel happiest regardless of the success of Take That. For the moment that place is Manchester, England. I live in a one bedroom apartment. It's really small, just big enough for me. It's got a brown and cream living room and cream bedroom plus a tiny kitchen. I'm very happy with it."

on love: "I have to hold back from developing any strong feelings for a girl. I get attached very easily but because of my job I have to hold back. 'Just keep it nice and casual', that's my rule."

on wanting to manage bands: "It would have to be a rock or grunge group because you get far too much flak with a pop band. Anything alternative and miserable will do so long as they don't smile too much."

on his luck: "I should be working as a labourer and married off to a girl in Manchester right now, but the chance has come along and I'm not going to waste it."

on sleeping: "I mumble sometimes, though apparently once I suddenly shouted out, 'I've got long legs!' God knows why!"

on singing: "We've always said it's not a competition to see who can record the most lead vocals. It's who does the best job – they're all better than me."

on staying real: "We all know what's going on in the world. At least I do."

on religion: "I'm interested in Christianity and interested in Buddhism. You see, I think all of these are religions and are a way of life for people... but not for me."

on doing _Baywatch_: "I'm not into Pamela Anderson. I'm not that into plastic!"

on his riches: "Let's put it this way, it doesn't hurt my pocket when I take all my friends out to dinner and pay for it all."

on his social life: After dinner I love going to the cinema, and after that, if I'm feeling fit enough, we'll go to a club. For good clubbing, my motto is the more the merrier. I prefer going to places where the music is dead funky rather than techno."

on the nice parts of fame: "I bought my mum a house!"

"I should be working as a labourer and married off to a girl in Manchester right now..."

on marriage: "I think a lot about getting married. I might have already met the person I want to spend the rest of my life with and not known it."

on singing: "When I was having my singing lessons recently I bought some Karaoke tapes. I was sat in my bedroom with my mic singing along... oh that's really embarrassing."

on the end: "I'd like to go out on top. I'd hate us to call it a day when we're unsuccessful — we'd be a laughing stock."

on his feminine side: "I think I know how to work a camera, I think I have a feminine side from spending time with my sister as well... I used to think I'd look quite good as a girl. I have very feminine hands, they're very thin and girlie."

on crying: "I do cry. It's healthy. I was at home in bed about a month ago. I just fancied crying. I feel better for it."

on wishes: "I've got a local pub and I haven't been in it for four years and I keep thinking, 'Right, one of these days.' But you know what I'd really like to do? I'd like to get a rail card and go away for three months with a rucksack on my back and just doss it — sit around fires and have sing-songs with guitars."

on his role in Take That: "I only saw myself being a back seater in this band, but I've probably had more covers than any of the others. I get sick of seeing my own pigging face on telly or on magazine covers!"

on recording Nobody Else: "The best thing about recording the album was that we did it up north — most of it was recorded at Gary's house. It was a bit like going to school really — we'd get there at 9 o'clock and finish at half three, then drive home! It was really relaxing — there was a lot of sunbathing in Gary's back garden."

on his image: "I am a nice guy. I'm not a pigging angel though."

on his talent: "I don't think I'm very talented. I just work hard at what I do."

on the fans: "Gary's writing may be maturing but it's a natural progression. We love our teen following and they still come to our concerts."

on success: "Look at us! Five years ago we were borrowing Jason's cycling shorts to go on stage. Now we're in Dolce and Gabbana."

on ambition: "Our aim now is the world."

mark

"I'm a nice guy. I'm not a pigging angel though."

Mark on Take That's success: "I think we're very lucky to have met Gary and held onto his hand, hahaha."

Gary on Take That's lucky break: "I used to play a bit of football as a kid, but, unlike Mark, I was usually in goal! I suppose there's a strong possibility that Take That may never have happened if Mark hadn't been injured. He could've been a Man United player by now instead!"

PJ Harvey on Take That: "I really like Take That. I'm into them, I watch the concerts on the telly. They're really good at what they do, and there are so many groups who are bad at what they do, you've got to admire them."

Mark on Take That chat: "The lads are the people I share my feelings with more than anyone else… We talk about pretty much everything."

Mark on Take That-induced insomnia: "If we've got tours coming up, I like to think of every song in my mind and picture what we can do with it. I always sound like I do a lot of worrying. I don't really — it's just organising things."

Shampoo on Take That: "Who's the coolest bod on the planet?" Jacqui: "Jason from Take That…" Carrie: "And Mark Owen's cool…"

Mark on looking after Take That: "I worry about the rest of the group. I'm always making sure everyone's got their bags and all their bits. I think it annoys the others."

Jason on Taking the strain: "If we're under pressure it's good to have Gaz there — I don't think he sees himself as a leader, but if there's a decision to be made, we all turn to Gaz."

Howard on a Take That surprise (the others arranged a stripogram for him): "I had to play the game and pretend I was enjoying myself, but in fact I WAS enjoying it."

Mark on Taking it easy: "You realise that your'e not going to please everybody, but we can't sit around and worry about it."

Gary on Taking the rough with the smooth: "Things do frustrate me — we get too busy for the really important things sometimes… But you can't win them all!"

Howard's mum on Howard: "He was always digging for treasure and would bring home the weirdest things. He was always filthy and never thought about washing his neck — until he started noticing girls, of course!"

eyewitness

Tom Howard – or "Smudger" as he's known by Take That – spent two months living, eating and partying with the boys when he joined them as official band photographer on their European Tour. Here he gives us the inside story of what it's like to be on the road with Jason, Gary, Howard, Mark and Robbie.

report

How did you get involved in the tour, Tom?

Via Lulu, oddly enough. I was doing a studio shoot with her and, of course, she's also managed by Take That's manager, Nigel Martin-Smith. I chatted with Nigel for around ten minutes – about what I'd done – and thought nothing more of it.

I'd met the lads a few times when I was an assistant for another photographer but hadn't actually worked with them on my own, so I was more surprised than anyone when Nigel asked around, took a good look at my work and then decided I was the man for the job!

What was it like when the tour started?

A bit nerve-wracking. I'd say all the lads were really apprehensive. When we were travelling to Rotterdam on March 15th the boys were all a bit like, 'Gawd. Hope all the rehearsals pay off! Do you think it'll be as good as we want it to be?'... that kind of thing. Of course, the first show was amazing.

I soon realized it was going to be intensely hard work. A typical day would be: travel in the morning and then get to the hotel, and then arrive at the show venue at 4 pm. At 4.15 the boys would soundcheck, then two of them would do a TV interview while the rest did a radio interview and then there'd be a press conference for the country's newspapers and magazines. Then the

Next thing I knew he was being rushed off stage. Seconds later a security guy ran around the stage and said, 'Tom, here! Quick!'

When I got around the back of the stage, Howard was lying on his back, obviously in agony, surrounded by paramedics. But Howard had pushed the pain to the back of his mind and got someone to come and get me so we could get pictures. A total professional!

Apart from the fact that all the lads insisted on calling me Smudger (press talk for "photographer") whenever I appeared ("Ey up! Here comes Smudger!"), they were all pretty well behaved.

If anyone was up for pranking it would be Robbie. We'd set up a brilliant portrait shot — a bit sultry — and just before I took the shot he'd whip off his T-shirt and pull faces (which often made a really cool pic, so I didn't mind in the least).

boys would *always* go backstage to meet and greet some fans (which of course they didn't have to but always insisted on doing), and then it'd be time to get changed so they could go on stage (with the rest of the crew doing the dance routines backstage!). They'd do all that work, come off stage at 11.30 and *then* they'd get some time to themselves. Since I had to be around at all times to take the shots, I worked the same hours!

What were the boys like to photograph?

The boys were brilliantly professional — completely up for photo opportunities. They really want the fans to get the best shots they can!

A major example of this was when Howard broke his finger on stage in Berlin. I was standing in the photographers' pit at the front taking shots, when I suddenly saw him do his usual back flip over Mark and then land really awkwardly on his hand. Snap. The finger went!

What was the actual travelling like?

The tour set-up was quite simple. There were two buses — one for the Take That band and one for Take That themselves. I travelled on either one depending on the schedule and general mood! Once on board it was just a case of relaxing until we arrived.

Everyone was into watching videos — Monty Python's *The Life Of Brian* seemed to be quite popular with the boys — and for a while all the lads were really into playing Super-Soccer on the Nintendo. Airports were really easy to contend with as well. When we arrived we'd find that security men had gone on ahead and got the tickets and seats sorted out and checked in all the baggage, so it was just a case of walking into the airport, through customs and straight to the departure gate.

The only time it went a bit wrong was when we were in Milan. Then I remember the police decided to drive us

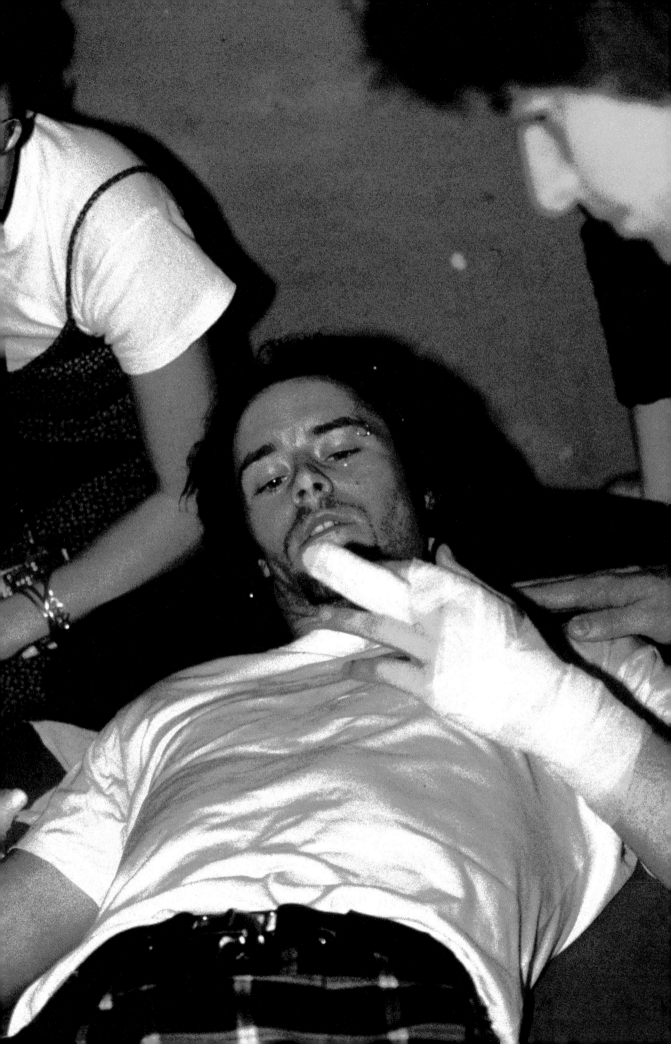

straight on to the tarmac for safety reasons (to protect the fans from a crush) and unfortunately all the security guys were waiting for us in the airport. Everyone was on their walkie-talkies going: 'Where are you?' 'In the airport! Where are you!??'

Did you get to hang out and relax with the boys?

We didn't get much time to ourselves, so when we did get moments during the day it was usually for cat-napping or maybe working out in a hotel gym, but, yeah, we hung out in the evenings when the boys really partied.

They'd come back after a show and if there was a disco or bar in the hotel, they'd all be down there — Robbie usually behind the bar playing at being a DJ and the rest of the lads dancing and socialising and having a good time.

They'd party until about 3 am and then it would be bed time. Me? I'd be there propping my eyes open. I don't know where they got the energy.

One pretty good night I remember was in the Hilton Hotel in Milan, which had a bowling alley in it, so we all went down and had a crack of it. Were they good? Er... I can safely say today that I taught Take That everything they know about ten pin bowling!"

Would you travel with Take That again?

In an instant. They're the nicest, most professional band I think I've worked with.

practice makes perfect

It might not seem like it, but even Take That need practice to be *that* perfect.

Howard: "How does the triple twist with the back flip combined with a semi-somersault go, Jason?"

Jason: "Er. Something like this?"

There are two things which we *definitely* know about Take That: Numero uno — they love performing live; and numero, er, two-o — they like their fans to get the best deals going.

So, as you can imagine, when it comes to touring — a time when both elements combine — the boys like to get it right. To them, giving the fans the best deal means putting on a spectacular show, which in turn means great performances and cunning dance routines.

To achieve their goals the boys take ages to finely tune their show and, once they've got it honed, turn to an old adage to keep them going: practice (and practice, and practice!) makes perfect.

Here are some scenes we captured from the strenuous rehearsals for 95's European Tour. You're looking at history in the making!

howard's end

To read the papers, you'd have thought he'd committed a dreadful crime — at least chanted satanic rites on stage or something...

"Cheeky devil!" screamed the *Daily Express.*

"Horny!" yelled the *Star.*

And the reason for such outrage?

A bum. A rather lovely bum, but a bum all the same. The bum in question belonged to Howard Donald, and was revealed in its full-moon glory when TT launched their nationwide tour back in 1994.

If you believed the tabloids (and we *all* believe the tabloids...) some parents dragged their kids screaming from auditoriums across the country because they thought Howard's behind was rather... er... forward for a pop concert in front of such innocent fans.

Hmm? With banners such as "Mark don't be silly, show us your willy" flying high in the crowds, some thought that TT needed to be protected from their fans, not t'other way around!

The band's comment on the furore? Over to Gary...

"None of us think our look or our stage gear is too raunchy for our young fans because it's all done for fun. Everything is done tongue in cheek." (Haw, haw.)

The general consensus? When Mr Donald dared to bare we got a bum deal... and LOVED it!

changes ⊞

It's hair today and gone tomorrow for the boys that like to keep a-head of the rest.

It's been a hairy old time for the That boys this annum. In the olden days, fashion pundits turned to them to grab trends for clobber. Now, it seems, another set of style-seekers are turning to the lads for inspiration: the barnet bunch are checking out TT's bonces!

Yup, following Robbie's phenomenal winning of the "Best Haircut" award at the *Smash Hits* Poll Winners' Party, Take That's hair-dos have been attracting even more attention than usual.

Howard, of course, went for his wild man of rock look with his DIY super-cool dreads (he's probably one of the first men in history to actually dreadlock his beard).

Mark and Jason went for shag hairdos of various lengths (Mark's in particular seemed to spring up and down like a yo-yo). And Gary? Well he stuck with what suited him, his cool crop.

So, as you can see, with Take That's hair-dos "Everything Changes but Gary"... but he's perfect already, so it's just the way we like it!

You think you don't know him, in fact you're *positive* you haven't seen him — but you're wrong: Morgan Penn, the artist drafted in by TT to design the sleeve of their latest album, *Nobody Else*, is a bit of a star in his own right.

Remember those TV ads on Channel 4 in which a gold-painted bald bloke looked into the camera and winked? That was Morgan! And remember the Vauxhall ad starring all the supermodels in which Naomi Campbell blasted a man tied to a metal torture device? Yup! Morgan too!

Morgan is an all round artist and impressed the boys with his album cover ideas because they had the feel of a Buddhist alter (and the boys have quite an affinity with the East as you know).

"At first the plan was to set up the alter with the boys themselves super-imposed in the middle of it, but as soon as

The Dalek toothbrush holder: "A 'Gary's childhood' thing — he probably used this to get rid of the sherbet."

The Book: "It's called *The Art Of Wisdom* and Mark was heavily into it at the time of the shoot. It's full of philosophical type sayings. Mark seems an introspective kinda guy!"

The Sherbet: "A favourite Gary Barlow pick-me-up apparently."

The Pouch: "Odd this one. It belongs to Robbie and he's had it for ages but he doesn't know what's in it and won't look. We had a feel and we think it's either a baby tooth or a pearl."

The Car: "When we were doing the first shoot, Jason was like, 'Top! Can I send you down a replica of my new car?', and so he faked this one up. I've no idea what his car actually is, but if it's *exactly* like this one he's in trouble!"

The Tetley T Man: "This was in the original shoot but Jason was like, 'Top! We love tea! Leave that in!'"

art on yo

"I met 'em I knew there wasn't a chance of that," Morgan laughs.

"They did *not* want to be on the cover. Like Jason said at the time, 'People know what we look like so let's give 'em something else.' The dolls did the trick."

"The shot which appears on the cover is actually the second shoot we did. First time around I set up the 'alter' with bits and pieces that I thought represented the band and the lads came in half way through and were like, 'Great!'

"Suddenly everyone was full of ideas, went away and then sent a big box down from their office in Manchester with bits and pieces in it, each representing themselves. Hence shoot two! "Mark was probably the most enthusiastic. He wrote out this huge list explaining what everything meant to which band member. He was completely brilliant."

The Mirror at the back: "Yeah! That's the boys. On a larger version you can see objects behind the dolls reflected in the mirror, and if you look very closely you might make out a Port Vale mascot. Guess whose idea that was?!"

The Buddha: "This is Jason's. I believe he picked it up in Japan and loves it because his first visit there was pretty precious to him!"

The Letter Blocks: "When you pull 'em out of the picture and arrange them in the right order they spell 'Take That'."

The Clowns: "Each one is meant to represent a different member of the band. Don't ask me which. I've been told I've got to work it out myself."

The Bracelet: "This belongs to the invincible, God-like icon Adam Ant. He came into the studio while we were doing the shoot and said 'Take That? Great! I'm a fan!', and gave us his bracelet. The boys were well impressed! Geezer!"

The Silver Dolphin: "Yeah, it's Mark's. It represents his tattoo."

⊕

Take That, Take That and ... er, Take That. Yep, 1995

Spooky fact: when a pneumatic drill is going at its ultimate loudest, it manages to scream out an amazing 100 decibels of sound. Loud, right?

So you can imagine why the organisers of the *Smash Hits* Poll Winners' Party were freaked-out when they realised that the screams for multi-winners Take That were so loud that they ploughed out an unbelievable 115.3 decibels of noise.

The fans could be forgiven. They had a lot to scream about.

Our boys managed to scoop up not one, not two but — get this — **seven** awards at the *Smash Hits* do:

They grabbed 1994 Best Group, Best British Group, Best Single *(Sure)*, Best Pop Video *(Sure)*, Best Dressed Person (Mark Owen), Most Fanciable Star (Mark Owen) and — most important this — Best Haircut (Robbie Williams).

The awards didn't stop there. The last 12 months have been totally trophy-filled for Take That! Having "walked" the *Smash Hits* awards in Britain, they proved their metal in Europe, earning themselves the "Best Group" award at the MTV awards, which took place at

clear major mantel space.

a swanky do at Berlin's Brandenburg Gate.

Final awards news is that if Gary Barlow plays his cards right he might grab the biggest award of all: as if an Ivor Novello wasn't enough, Mr Barlow currently has a league of fans lobbying parliament, demanding that our Gazza be given a peerage (ie made Sir Gary Barlow!)

The Big Breakfast has been backing the campaign (primarily launched by the Harms family from Northwich — geezers!).

As a show spokesman said: "An official form has been filled in and viewers are being urged to send letters to John Major backing the request."

It may not have happened yet but time is on Gazza's side.

Take That: they're an award-winning bunch, and worth every trophy, we'll warrant!

So you think you know Take That, huh? Sure, you know the truth behind that 'Jason and Karen-from-*The-Living-Soap*' story, and maybe have the griff on Gary's quest for love. But do you know the *real* TT details? **Test your knowledge and see...**

the TT quiz

1) Which member wants to name his boy kids Sam, Ben or Brent?
   a) Howard.
   b) Robbie.
   c) Mark.

2) Who was it that quit Take That for a couple of days early on in his career because he couldn't take the pressure of being a teen idol?
   a) Gary.
   b) Jason.
   c) Robbie.

3) Mark's motto is 'Carpe Diem' taken from his favourite movie *Dead Poets Society*. What does it mean?
   a) 'Body and Soul.'
   b) 'Fish come and go' (as in 'Plenty more fish in the sea'!).
   c) 'Seize the day.'

4) Gary had to stop karate lessons as a teenager 'cause he kept breaking his fingers (not great for playing piano), but which of these accolades did he earn when he was still chopping at 13?
   a) He managed to beat the world champion.
   b) He was the second youngest second dan black belt!
   c) He was on Children's BBC talking about what a brilliant sport it is.

5) Which member of Take That once admitted to having dreams about beating up one of the other members of the band?
   a) Jason.
   b) Howard.
   c) Gary.

6) **Why was Jason Orange brought up not drinking alcohol or coffee?**

   a) He's allergic to them.

   b) He doesn't like them.

   c) He was brought up as a strict Mormon.

7) **How many hit singles had Take That had by the time they put out *Sure*?**

   a) 11.

   b) 14.

   c) 18.

10) **In March '94 Mark had to have medical treatment for dehydration. How did he become so ill?**

   a) A bit too much of the old fall-y down water, if you get our drift...

   b) Dancing too hard and forgetting to drink 'eau!

   c) He spent too long in the sauna!

8) **Which top hairdresser was responsible for Howard's dread-locked look?**

   a) Terence Renati (who also does Dannii Minogue's hair).

   b) No one. He did it himself.

   c) Nicky Clarke, Hairdresser to The Stars!

9) **Which artist does Gary Barlow reckon he likes to 'snog' to?**

   a) Björk.

   b) Prince.

   c) Lionel Richie.

how did ya fare?

10-30 Fan? Erm... hate to be rude here, but are you *truly* a Take That fan? Seems to us you need to catch up on some of the basic essentials here. Now let's start at the beginning: Robbie beat 2,000 people in auditions to become a member of Take That. Jason supports Manchester United football team and Mark's piano teacher was Polish. Go study!

40-60 Fan-Tastic No one could ever call you a fair-weather fan! You know that Howard wants a St Bernard dog and Robbie's fave soap is *Coronation Street*, but you're not too hot on the deep, psychological details. A little more devotion and a bit of research and you *could* be a contender for the number one fan.

70-100 Fan-Atical! Crikey! You're obsessed! We bet you know that Gary used hypnosis to rid himself of his fear of cars, don't you?! Bet you also know that Robbie's dummy sucking started when he wanted to hide a spot! You love Take That above and beyond the call of duty and deserve to be known as a superfan!

"Take That..." (stated manager Nigel Martin-Smith, earlier last year) "reign supreme in Europe, Pacific Asia and Latin America."

He wasn't lying!

A quick flick through the band's press cuttings is proof enough that the lads are an international force to be reckoned with.

Headlines ranging from "Sianara Robbie" to "Italian Stallions" relay glamorous reports from across the globe detailing TT's high jinks in Europe and beyond.

When Mark and co. picked up the MTV award for best band in '95, it was definite evidence that they had pushed their perimeters further than Blighty's shores.

Yep. Milan, Paris, Tokyo, Berlin... Take That rule 'em all. But there's one "small" country the band have yet to crack...

The U.S. of A.

Mid 1995, some sceptical journalists started scare-mongering and suggested that it might be too late for Take That to Take America. The same journalists said that Take That were a purely European phenomenon, that Americans wouldn't "get it" and revealed to the world that RCA in the US had decided not to press *Nobody Else*, but had told Take That they were free to take it to another record company.

It was true that Hollywood had been calling for Robbie to take up some film roles... and *Baywatch* mogul David Hasselhoff had signed a deal with the lads to star in a one-off Miami episode of his soap in 1996.

But was this enough?

In a letter to the record industry paper *Music Week* from his offices in South King Street, Manchester, Take That manager

Nigel Martin-Smith reassured the fans: "I do know what I'm doing with regards to the US," he said. "The *Baywatch* appearance was announced to generate publicity for the new single (then *Back For Good!*) while the band were out of the country, but it is not the only confirmed move. It's just a piece of a jigsaw that I am putting together that will see Take That break in the States."

In other words… watch this space!

Whether Take That take Manhattan or not, one thing's for sure; their quest for Stateside fame will at least bond them together for a few more years

The band had revealed to Andy Coulson of the *Sun* that they had considered splitting up back in January '95 because they thought their time in the limelight was fading and wanted to quit at the top.

And, as Mark concludes:

"Four years ago we only saw the world as Manchester, then we saw it as Britain and now it literally is the world. We have to try our luck in America or we'll regret it for the rest of our lives…"

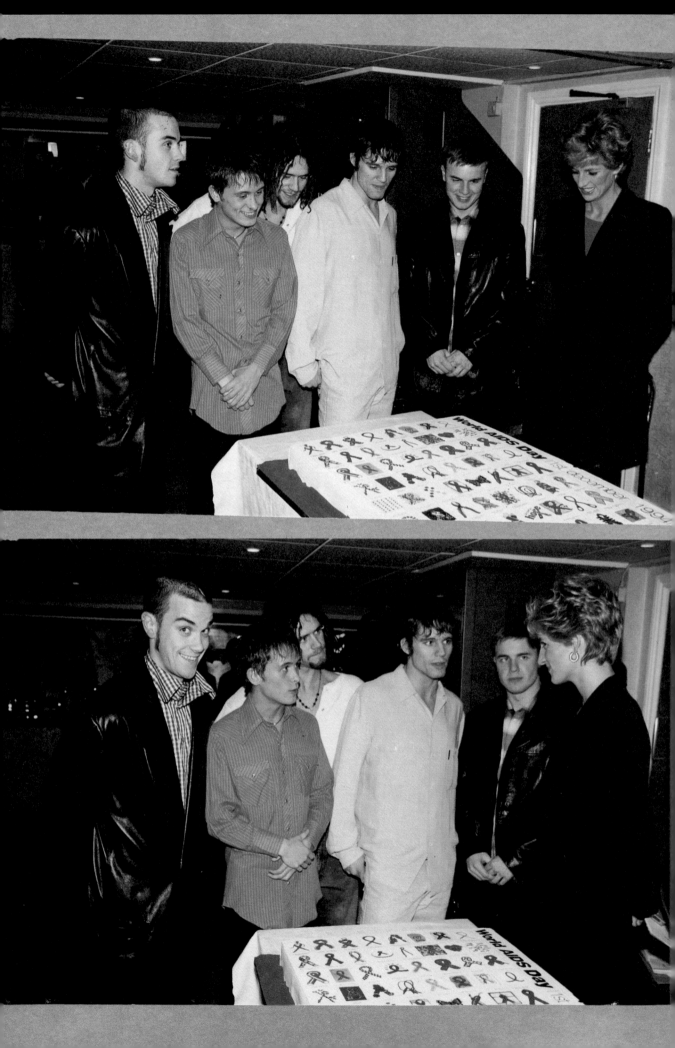

a royal affair

What happened when the Princes of Pop met the Prince and Princess of Wales?

Any Thatter worth their salt knows that Jason Orange – crowned prince of torso twists and back flips – has Royal Blood.

Jason is a direct descendant of King William of Orange, a regal geezer who held the British throne in the 17th century and was also a member of the Dutch royal family.

That said, most of us were less than surprised when the company of all five Take Thatters was requested by royalty this year and were *forced* to go to some very la-di-da gigs.

The most amazing one was when Princess Diana invited the lads to tea to thank them for agreeing to front her *Concert of Hope* on World Aids Day.

As the fearless five sat and sipped tea with her, Mark – never backwards at coming forwards – piped up:

"Are you free on Sunday? Fancy going out?"

Mark has always said he fancied Di and had pledged that he'd ask her out if ever he met her. Unfortunately Di turned him down (is she maad?). She grinned and said, "Sorry, I'm afraid I'm busy. But thanks for asking."

Mark apparently shrugged and said, "That's a shame."

The That boys' second encounter with royalty was with Di's estranged husband Charles at The Royal Variety Performance. The future king wasn't as clued up about Take That as Di was and had to ask who it was who wrote the songs, before walking all the way back up the line to our Gary.

Our lads were said to be "thrilled" at having met the possible future King and Queen of England... but not as thrilled, we reckon, as Chuck and Di were at meeting The Undisputed Princes of Pop!

the day after today

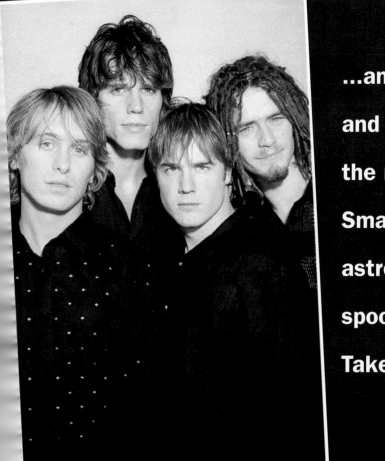

...and the next
and the next and
the next. *Elektra*,
Smash Hits'
astrologer, takes a
spooky peek into
Take That's future.

Born: 20.1.71   Star-sign: Capricorn

His personality: On the day Gary was born, the Sun and Mercury were in Capricorn and the Moon and Mars were in Scorpio, making him the definite leader of the band. He's very optimistic, strong and positive and great at making plans, but may be prone to excessive worrying. The Sun/Moon combination means he's a bit materialistic. Venus in Sagittarius means he's friendly and loves a chat! If he wasn't in Take That, he'd make a good caterer, detective or doctor!

His year ahead: Changes are afoot in November, when Gary concentrates less on his work and puts some effort into getting out and about. Less nights in writing songs and more nights out on the razzle! From January '96, his personal horizons are broadening (and his waistline may be expanding too if he's not careful!). April '96 is a landmark month for Gary, because that's when he really starts heading for superstardom. And it seems America is a-beckoning...

gary barlow

Born: 10.7.70 Star-sign: **Cancer**

jason orange

His personality: Three planets – the Sun, Mercury and Mars – were in Cancer on the day of Jason's birth, and the Moon was in Virgo. This means Jason is hard-working and co-operative, but may have workaholic tendencies. Because he allows his heart to rule his head, he could get into lots of trouble. Venus in Leo makes him big-hearted and immensely kind. In love, he needs a partner who gives as much as they take. He's a showy person and if he wasn't in Take That, he'd be a good actor, film director or politician!

His year ahead: Before Christmas this year, Jason decides to make more effort with his work and could well be penning the band's new year hit. After that, he may consider jacking in the whole thing to go in pursuit of something he considers less frivolous. Destiny sees him presenting a TV documentary over the next year, working with a film producer on an epic production. By Easter next year, the stars predict that he may not be in Take That any more, but could be pursuing his dream...

mark owen

Born: 27.1.74 Star-sign: Aquarius

His personality: The Sun, Mercury and Venus were in Aquarius and the Moon was in Pisces on the day Mark was born, and this means he's sexy and creative. He's a bit impressionable and can be self-indulgent, spending much of his time in his own little fantasy world. He's a great mate and would go out of his way to help a friend in need. Mars in Taurus makes him hard-working and very trustworthy. If he wasn't a member of Take That, he'd make a good builder, footballer or estate agent.

His year ahead: Mark may have some personal difficulties to deal with in the coming few months, but by the start of 1996, when his ruling planet Uranus enters Aquarius, he'll have got on top of things. What he'll need more than anything from that month onwards is freedom and it seems he could be making a big break from the past. If anyone hopes to marry him in the coming year, forget it. Mark's his own man for some time yet.

His personality: On Howard's birthday, the Sun, Moon, Mercury and Mars were all in Taurus, making him strong-willed, cheerful, sociable and fun-loving. It's the Sun/Moon combination which gives him his musical talents. He loves learning and hates it when he comes across things he can't understand. He's quite opinionated and dislikes being contradicted. Venus in Aries means he's the passionate type, who falls in love quickly. If he wasn't in Take That, he'd do well as a builder, farmer or photographer.

His year ahead: Love is in the air right now, and although Howard likes to keep his love-life to himself, things get so passionate around Christmas time that there's no way he can keep it secret. The love affair could be with another celebrity and could cause a bit of a stir in Starville. This only serves to propel Howie to the heights of superstardom as he and his paramour adorn the front page of every newspaper in the land. It could all be a storm in a teacup and the big romance could be over before the year is out.

never forget

Throughout the evening, news flashes on national television and radio networks told the public what few had suspected and none wanted confirmed: Robbie Williams had left Take That; the reason given was that he could no longer give the long-term commitment the band needed.

Robbie's departure means Take That will now become the 'Fab Four' instead of the 'Fab Five'. The other members of the band insist they will carry on performing as Take That and that the split was amicable.

Although the news that Robbie was leaving left most feeling a tad sombre, the band feel more committed then ever.

"When Robbie first announced that he wanted to leave, of course we were all devastated and did even think about splitting up. But we love what we do so much and have so much to look forward to with the new single and tour, tours in Australia and the Far East and the release of *Back for Good* in the States, that we feel we couldn't possibly call it a day." Mark.

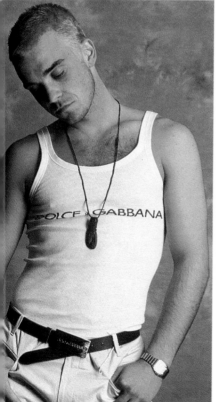

Jason reinforces the view: "We'll all miss Rob, but we feel that the only way to go now is forward."

Gary agrees: "The four of us are still 100% committed to this band and are very much looking forward to a long future together."

The band's new single *Never Forget* is an apt and fitting tribute to the success of the band: "We've come so far and we've reached so high... but we're still so young and we hope for more..."

Robbie Williams will be missed. No-one can be really sure of his plans, but one thing we can count on is that he'll retain his upbeat sense of humour that made him such an integral part of Take That for so long!